Object Logos

A handbook of object
marks of identity, compiled
& edited by Counter-Print.

T0349817

With special thanks to all
the contributors for their
support, time and talent.

ISBN 978-1-915392-09-1

**Blended
Learning &
Study Center**

Educational
courses,
programs
& services

2016

Ben Loiz Studio
benloiz.com

Mariano
Lampacrescia
dribbble.com/
mareanx

RIF

Non-profit
children's literacy
organisation

2011

Mother Design
motherdesign.com

Michinokichi   Kokugakuin   2017   6D
University   6d-k.com
reading initiative

Kokugakuin Book Project

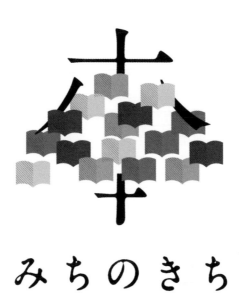

MagazineWorks Custom publishing consultants 2003 Alexander Isley Inc.
alexanderisley.com

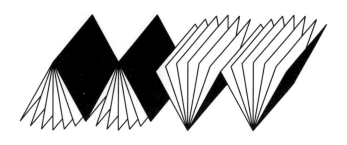

Toilet Roll For Seki, a printing company 2021 Grand Deluxe
grand-deluxe.com

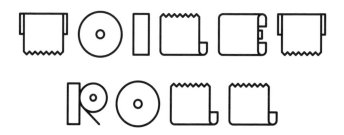

**Sole Time
Kicks**

Footwear

2022

The Studio Temporary
thestudiotemporary.
com

Terri Timely   Directors of   2016   Bedow
music videos   bedow.se
& commercials

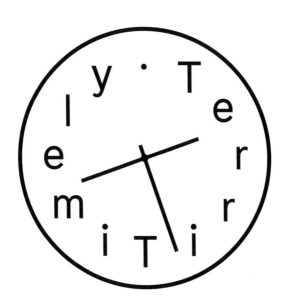

D'Angelo Coffee

Woodstock Coffee Co.

Beverage

2020

The Studio Temporary
thestudiotemporary.
com

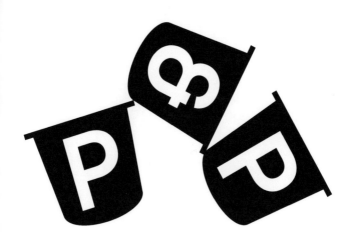

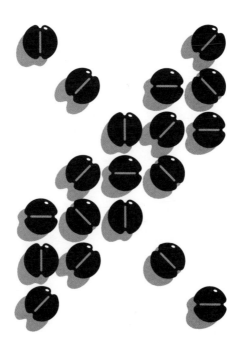

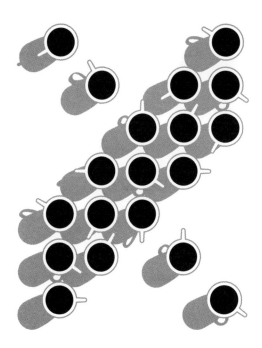

sojourn pottery

Social Studies   Collection of   2017   Civilization
objects created   builtbycivilization.
for Open-Editions   com

**Ceremony
Matcha**

Matcha

2019

Alphabet
madebyalphabet.
com

CEREMONY

MATCHA
抹茶

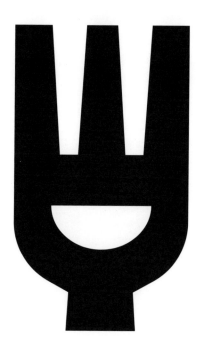

Swedish Tapas   Tapas bar with   2022   Jesper Holm
                    a Swedish touch,   Designstudio
                    located in Spain   jesperholm.se

Unikitch   Industrial   2019   Toormix
               products for   toormix.com
               kitchen utilities

**Design
Lecture Series**

Non-profit design 2013
lecture series

Civilization
builtbycivilization.
com

Civilization
builtbycivilization.
com

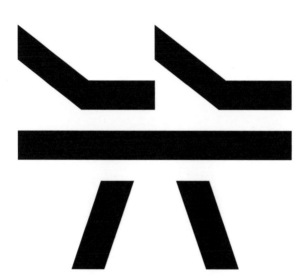

MAT
MISJONEN

EST. 1823

Kerry Daynes Forensic   2006   MARK Studio
                   psychology

THE
CERIPH
MENTORSHIP
PROGRAMME

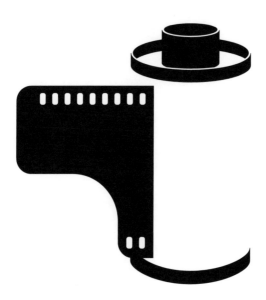

Andorra Kid's Film Festival   Film, music & contemporary arts festival   2018   Familia byfamilia.com

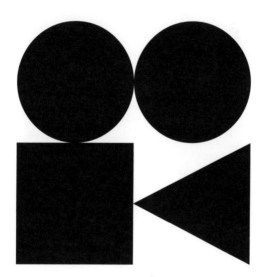

BioVideo Record a baby's 2014 Anagrama
first moments anagrama.com

Local Film production 2019 Mariano
Productions company Lampacrescia
dribbble.com/
mareanx

**Charles
Parker Trust**

Radio &
broadcast charity

2017

Supple Studio
supple.studio

**Opelika
Songwriters
Festival**

Music festival   2019

The Studio Temporary
thestudiotemporary.
com

Casey
Record Fair

·Record fair

2019

Steve Gavan
stevegavan.work

The Sound Wall Jazz Series   Music festival   2022   The Studio Temporary
thestudiotemporary.com

AbemaTV   Online talkshow   2018   Airside Nippon
airside.jp

THE HOLD
BY REVELRY BREWING
CHARLESTON SC

**Made in
the USA**

Fishing

2021

The Studio Temporary
thestudiotemporary.
com

Proudly Made in the USA

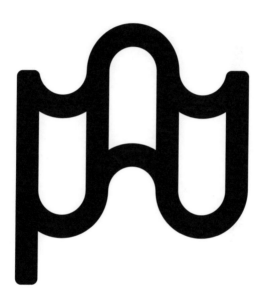

Studio
Jens Assur

Photography /
film production

2009

BankerWessel
bankerwessel.com

STUDIO JENS ASSUR

| **Cafe Club** | Cafe & sandwich shop | 2021 | The Click theclickdesign.com |

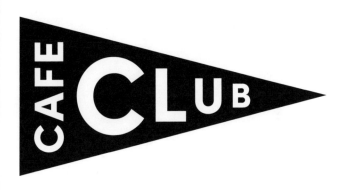

| **Sherpa GX** | Travel agency | 2023 | leolab leolab.mx |

| **Meta** | Tech company | 2020 | ITAL/C |
| | | | italic-studio.com |

| **Padel Haus NYC** | Padel club | 2022 | leolab |
| | | | leolab.mx |

Le Ballon d'Or   Annual football   2019   République Studio
award presented   republique.studio
by magazine
France Football

**Play Soccer
to Give**

Non-profit
organisation
using soccer for
social change

2013

Chris Rushing
chrisrushing.com

NCFA   Governing   2012   JB Studio
body of football   jb-studio.co.uk
in Norfolk

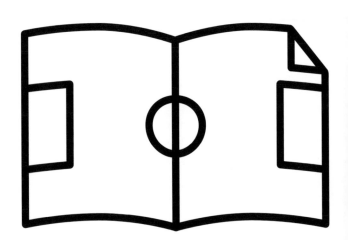

Hiroshi Bros.
Skate & Supply

Sports

2020

The Studio Temporary
thestudiotemporary.
com

Sneaker Shoe / 2017 Jay Fletcher
clothing store jfletcherdesign.com

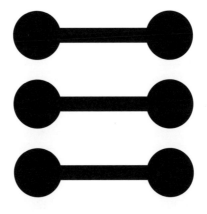

Green Laces

Fused & Bruised
Recordings /
DJ Scissorkicks

Music artist

1999

Zip Design
zipdesign.co.uk

Weargame /
Game Paused

Game Paused
exhibition / show

2005

Zip Design
zipdesign.co.uk

Parasol

Events

2016

Richard Robinson
Design
richardrobinson
design.co.uk

Homegrown Homesewn

Sewing / quilting shop

2021

Jay Fletcher
jfletcherdesign.com

Nordic House   Dry-cleaning shop   2013   Anagrama
anagrama.com

Ninety   Hair stylist   2006   MARK Studio
markstudio.co.uk

**Homegrown
Homesewn**

Sewing /
quilting shop

2021

Jay Fletcher
jfletcherdesign.com

旭屋朝日

Asahiya Asahi

Homegrown Homesewn   Sewing / quilting Shop   2021   Jay Fletcher
jfletcherdesign.com

Homegrown Homesewn   Sewing / quilting Shop   2021   Jay Fletcher
jfletcherdesign.com

**Barber
Money Joc**

Barber

2021

The Studio Temporary
thestudiotemporary.
com

サロン美容室

**Merchants of
Good Fortune –
Merchants
Tavern**

Casual dining   2012

StudioSmall
studiosmall.com

Kindo

Boutique for
kids' clothing
& accessories

2015

Anagrama
anagrama.com

KINDO

SHOP

FOR THE LITTLE ONES

Luxury Presence   Creative agency   2017   The Branding People
                     for real estate   tbp.studio
                     agencies

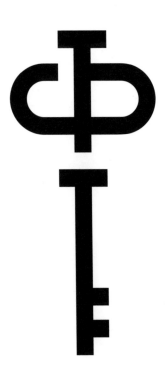

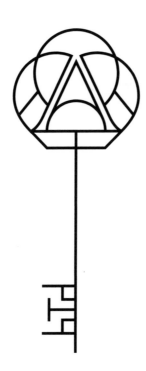

Naked Tech /
Naked Wines

Technology /
development
department
of Naked Wines

2021

JB Studio
jb-studio.co.uk

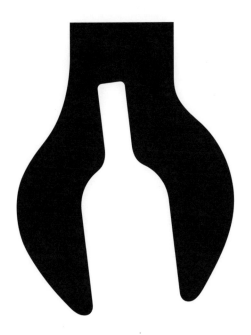

| **Hatlanta** | Manufacturing | 2019 | The Studio Temporary thestudiotemporary. com |

| **Fastener World** | Fasteners vender | 2011 | Maksim Arbuzov maksimarbuzov.com |

Upcycle
Recordings

Independent
record label

2020

Zip Design
zipdesign.co.uk

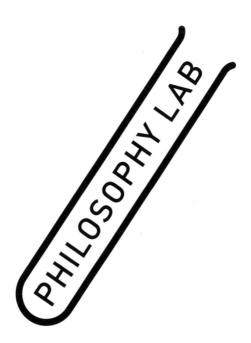

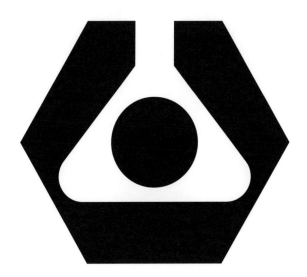

Grits & Grids Podcast 2018 The Studio Temporary
thestudiotemporary.
com

Editorial Portatil Publisher 2004 David Torrents
torrents.info

Botchan
Electric Power
Electricity
company
2018
Grand Deluxe
grand-deluxe.com

**Dantech
Electrical**

Industrial
electricians

2015

Jamie Fox
jamiefoxdesigner.
com

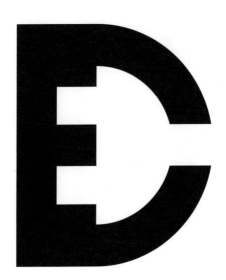

**Bulgarian
Television**

Television

1959

Stefan Kanchev
stefankanchev.com

Index of Companies

Object Logos

Compiled and edited
by Counter-Print
counter-print.co.uk

Designed by Jon Dowling
& Céline Leterme

First Published in 2023

Copyright © Counter-Print

ISBN 978-1-915392-09-1

Printed in China